Prairie Schooner Book Prize in Poetry | EDITOR: Kwame Dawes

Reliquaria

R. A. VILLANUEVA

University of Nebraska Press · Lincoln and London

Library of Congress
Cataloging-in-Publication Data
Villanueva, R. A.
[Poems. Selections]
Reliquaria / R. A. Villanueva.
pages   cm.
(Prairie Schooner book prize in poetry)
ISBN 978-0-8032-9638-1 (pbk.: alk. paper)
ISBN 978-0-8032-7650-5 (epub)
ISBN 978-0-8032-7651-2 (mobi)
ISBN 978-0-8032-7652-9 (pdf)
I. Title.
PS3622.I49395R45 2014
811'.6—dc23
2014008810

Set in Scala by Renni Johnson.
Designed by A. Shahan.

for Jennifer—
Friend, Everything

CONTENTS

3

ACKNOWLEDGMENTS

Many thanks to the editors of the following journals, in which these poems appear, sometimes in different forms:

AGNI: "Swarm"
Bellevue Literary Review: "Divination"
The Collagist: "Corpus," "Traps," and "What the bones tell us"
Crab Orchard Review: "All Souls' Day" and "Mine will be a beautiful service"
DIAGRAM: "These Bodies Lacking Parts"
Gulf Coast: "Antipodal"
Indiana Review: "Fish Heads"
Lantern Review: "Vanitas"
Letters: A Journal of the Yale Institute of Sacred Music: "God Particles"
The Literary Review: "Blessing the Animals," "Drifting toward the bottom, Jacques Piccard recalls the sky," and "Telemachy"
Ninth Letter: "Aftermaths" and "Sacrum"
Painted Bride Quarterly: "As the river crests, mud-rich with forgotten things" and "Confluences"
Smartish Pace: "After this, Loving Kindness and Asanga flew" and "Socorro"
Virginia Quarterly Review: "In Memory of Xiong Huang"
Washington Square: "In the dead of winter we"

"Drifting toward the bottom, Jacques Piccard recalls the sky" also appears in *A Face to Meet the Faces: An Anthology of Contemporary Persona Poetry* (University of Akron Press, 2012), edited by Stacey Lynn Brown and Oliver de la Paz.

"These Bodies Lacking Parts" also appears in *McSweeney's Internet Tendency*.

"Aftermaths" was originally written and performed for *Together We Are New York: Asian Americans Remember and Re-Vision 9/11*, a collaborative, community-based project cosponsored by Kundiman and the Lower Manhattan Cultural Council.

Special thanks to G. C. Waldrep, who selected "Aftermaths" and "Sacrum" as winners of the 2013 *Ninth Letter* Literary Award for poetry. For their faith in this book and in me: heartfelt gratitude to Kwame Dawes and the dedicated staff of *Prairie Schooner*/University of Nebraska Press.

Relentless thanks to my friends—mentors, all: Sarah Gambito, Joseph O. Legaspi, Oliver de la Paz, Vikas Menon, Jennifer Chang, Carolyn Micklem, Rick Barot, Aimee Nezhukumatathil, John Pineda, Patrick Rosal, Hossannah Asuncion, Kelly Zen-Yie Tsai, and the ever-growing, ever-powerful Kundiman family; Gina Apostol, Laurel Fantauzzo, Luis H. Francia, Nita Noveno, Bino A. Realuyo, Ricco Siasoco, and Lara Stapleton, a *barkada* to be reckoned with; Brandon Relucio; Oscar Bermeo and Barbara Jane Reyes; Paolo Javier; Eduardo C. Corral; Roger Bonair-Agard, Lynne Procope, and the louderARTS Project; Ken Chen and the Asian American Writers' Workshop; Gerald Maa and *The Asian American Literary Review*; Colin Cheney, Jessica Flynn, Ishion Hutchinson, Janine Joseph, Dante Micheaux, Bryan Patrick Miller, John Murillo, Mrigaa Sethi, Amber West, Adam Wiedewitsch, Ronnie Yates, and all my brilliant NYU compatriots and colleagues.

I am forever indebted to the wisdom and guidance of my teachers: Mr. Harry Dawson, Mr. Richard Binkowski, and Mr. Joseph Neglia; Pat C. Hoy and Darlene Forrest; Robin Becker, Breyten Breytenbach, Anne Carson and Robert Currie, Mark Doty, Eamon Grennan, Kimiko Hahn, Phillis Levin, Sharon Olds, Matthew Rohrer, and Sonia Sanchez.

For their love, support, and stories, a deep, resounding *salamat* to my family—immediate and extended, here and abroad. To Mom and Dad, Joanne and John, Rommel and Nina and Pterodactyl, to Tita Yoly, the Villanueva, Sotto, Sanchez, and Guadarrama families: thank you. To the Reyes (and Gohde), Cancio (and Potavin), de Vries, Goetz (and Gonzalez), and Velez families, and to the Mahjong Crew with all its new generations: thank you.

And, yes, to Jennifer: thank you, again and always.

Above all, undying love and respect to my grandparents, Dominador and Socorro Villanueva, who wanted and gave and worked for a better life.

RELIQUARIA

Sacrum

Though lacking the breadth
and mass of the iliac wing,
this sacred bone remains,
for Vesalius, broad as *hunger*,
as *grand and spacious*

as the sea. But he leaves names
and reasons for others, wants
only the seven figures of the thorax,
cares more about the *Cartilages*
of the Rough Artery.

He does not mention how this holy
place, cut from the ox-calf wrapped
in fat, was Achilles' mourning offering,
how the blessed ram, shank broken
over the fire, was Abraham's sacrifice

after his son. When I think aloud,
Nothing we do living
can be as beautiful
as what the living will do
with our bones, you reply

with ceremony, recounting
cremations from your childhood:
boys at pyre's base sifting through ash
for that fragment of sternum
which resembles a man

lost in meditation, those shards of hip
worthy of marigolds and hand-thrown urns
to set upon the Ganges. Years later
you find yourself home, on the edge
of a Greater Bangkok throttled

with fires and protest tambourines.
There amid talk of the hereafter
and makeshift triggers, you tend
to a lung bruised through the cage
of the ribs, send photos of Varanasi,

its bargefields and silks, a barber
drawing his knife across the cheeks
of the dead and their brothers.
What I have yet to show you back
is Sta. Rita de Cascia, its reliquary

chapel overtaken by flowers, this
grave mason preparing a space
for my grandfather as we watch
the youngest girls of the *barangay*
lifted up and passed, kicking

at the air, over the face of his casket.
Someone whispers, *So that his spirit
will keep to heaven*, and then I know
I am not entirely here: I stare
as a boy trowels earth into a paste

of mortar and spit; I hear Vesalius
take his artists to the head and
its moveable sutures, the bulwark
of temples made for *the soft nerves,
formed for the sake of the eyes*; I kneel

beside priests burning camphor
upon the ghats, brace this eldest son
for what he must break with his hands
and the sight of his father's soul
freed from the fabric of his skull.

1

From the beginning it has been end-conjuring.

JOSÉ GARCIA VILLA, *Doveglion*

Swarm

We were well down the ventral axis
      when Father Luke noticed. Our cuts
steady through the skin, our scalpels
      already through the thin give
of the sternum. With each bullfrog
      pinned to its block and double-
pithed by nail, he had by then
      talked us clean through the lungs,
past a three-chambered heart couched
      in tissue and vascular dye. We must
have been deeper among the viscera
      when he heard us laughing,
not at the swarm of black eggs
      spilling from the oviducts to
slime the cuffs of our blazers,
      but at a phallus, jury-rigged from
foil and rubber bands hanging off the crucifix,
      hovering above a chart of light-
independent reactions. This was nothing
      like the boys lowing through recitation
their antiphon for the layman whose wife
      we heard was trampled by livestock
over trimester break. Nothing at all
      like Sister Mary being made to face
the bathhouse scene from *Spartacus* in slow-
      motion or her freshmen rewinding again
and again stock films of chariot drivers pitched
      from their mounts, dragged
to their ends only to float backwards,
      hands bound up once more
in the reins. The Dean of Men confessed
      he knew of no prayer or demerit
that could redeem such disgrace,
      could conceive of no greater sin

against the Corpus. *Transgressors, all of you,*
        he said and closed the door behind him,
refusing to look at us or the thing
        that seemed to shimmer and twitch
with each frog's reflex kick against our forceps.
        He held us there far beyond
the last bell, waiting for just one among us
        to want forgiveness or for a single boy
to take back this mockery of the body
        our Lord had made.

Life Drawing

How she is quiet before his robe falls
each week to his ankles. This man who sits, nude
for my wife, whom she draws with Conté sticks

and pastel pencils. Each page in her notebook
is a parade of his torsos, galley proofs
of breastbones and chests. She explains

because these lines are my favorite
and shows me, traces with her knuckle tip
chin to sternum, jaw to shoulder, clavicle to cusp

of the arm. How in three passes
an artist makes a place for a head
to rest. Later, in blue and orange

pigments mixed at the edge of a knife, thinned
with linseed oil and mineral spirits,
my wife will paint him on a canvas

primed black. Again his body will end
just above the pelvis, will fade
into a fog of armrest or shadow, cushion

or hip as if rendered in some fugitive dye.
Because he is only the second man I have seen naked,
in person. His, just the third I have seen in my life.

When I tell my wife I want to write about her
naked, sketch her back's faint taper
as a class might to check perspective, describe

the moles I notice on the underside of a breast
as we make love, she says I can. And, in return,
she will paint the whole of me, bare

from the neck down as I pose
in our living room. *No one will even know*
this is you. The light will blank out your face.

These Bodies Lacking Parts

With raw sienna crushed by fist
in mortar, umber ground
to tender shadow to flesh,
Michelangelo binds a body,

mid-thrash, to the plaster,
its death flex throwing a heel
into the sheets, a bare arm
up at the drapery tempered

with cochineal red. In this Sistine
pendentive, Judith and her hand-
maid carry the artist's head away
on a dish, buckle at the knee

as if unable to bear fully the weight
of a skull hewn from the whole
of a man. On the mural opposite,
Michelangelo offers his skin

to the *Last Judgment*, hangs his face
elastic, lacking eyes or mass,
upon a martyr's fingertips. All
around the Redeemer, bodies vault

toward the clamor of heaven, plead
with their thresh and flail to render
themselves apart from the damned,
rowed toward a waiting maw.

••

These are the men Vesalius halves
and digs into: criminals fresh
from the Paduan gallows, gifts
of the executioner's axe. Unfolding

the heads of petty thieves, he laces
what nerves and veins he finds
within their sutures into a crown
shooting skyward. He figures

a new man from their bared
tributaries, writes of arteries
as latticework. When the anatomist
poses for his portrait, he instructs

apprentices to draw him directly
from nature, beside a body opened
at the wrist, his fingers gracing
the exposed vessels of the lower arm.

Telemachy

1.

Patron of the head
freed from the neck,
the new year's feasts
and burials,

martyr of good arms
      casting their stones,

benefactor of scattered wheals
like lagoons along the thigh,

      Saint Telemachus
bleed for us

into the arena floor,
its crushed sand, its lions halved.

2.

After first Communion I pose
by the sacristy, beneath a crucifix
of unfinished pine. I am wearing
a suit that rips at the armpits.

My father parts my hair to the left,
combs through with pomade,
presses down with his palms.

3.

My father never heard
of the Kill Sparrow War
in his province—

       Peking boys each morning
called to the nest-trees
with trumpets, their slingshots
aimed at the flocks,

red banners tied
to pots and spits. Knuckle-
bones into eggs, ladles
against prayer bells

and the birds

with nowhere to alight,
all falling from the sky
with little sound,

their hearts damp
fireworks going off
in their chests.

4.

Thoughtful-Telémakhos
knew nothing of scars

or the ramping boar, its tusk
caught in his father's leg,
above the knee just missing
the bone.

> What he knows
> are tremors.

His father's arms
pressed into his
before the Test.

His father's voice
a black ship
sealed with pitch.

5.

My father and his classmates
liked the air raid drills best
and would cheer the sirens
while they marched single-file
beneath the schoolhouse

posts. He imagined pilots
passing over the Philippine Sea,
scanning the open fields
for resistance, checking masks
for leaks, unable to read him

there in the dirt, flicking
anthills with his fingers,
pulling up grass by its roots.

Like when passing graveyards

We made sure to drive the length of the landfill with the windows shut
and the air circulation off. And each night we passed by these heaps

on the side of the highway afraid of breathing in. Off the muck
there was air Dad promised was safe. There were cattails thick like fingers

from the marsh grass, gulls in riot above the headshunts and exchange tracks.
At first sight of the Meadowlands, we sucked in through our mouths

and pinned our nostrils up with our wrists as long as our lungs could hold,
as though ghosts could seep through the soil, through coffins

and funeral dressings up and free of the sediment into the open sky.
Almost home, my brother told us about the Cemetery of the Holy Sepulchre

cut in half by the Parkway, about the bus driver who paid toll with gaskets
and reminded him to look out both sides, so he knew when it was over.

Fish Heads

Yanked free at the gills from cartilage and spine,
these fish heads my mother cleans, whose bodies she scales, throws
all into salt water and crushed tamarind. At dinner she alone
will spoon out their eyes with her fingers,

suck down each pair as we watch. *See, this is why the three of you
could never hide anything from me*—as though these organs
brought her sight to be soaked through the tongue.
When I tell her that I have tried to make this stew from memory,

she warns, *Don't waste what should be eaten.* Reminds me
of every delicate gift we have thrown away: tilapia stomach
best soured with vinegar, milkfish liver to melt
against the dome of the mouth. That after church,

a bucket of chicken soon became a blessing of wing gristle
and skin, dark meat no one else wanted to save. We refused
to taste her gizzards and hearts fried in fat, mocked
the smell of pig blood curdled on the stove, wished gone

her tripe steamed with beef bouillon and onion broth.
After my brother and sister push aside bowls of baby squid
in garlic ink, gag at my mention of ducks in their shells, boiled
alive in brine, my mother believes I was the only one to share

in such things. *Which maybe means,* she says, *in some former life
you and I were seabirds or vampires or wolves.*

In Memory of Xiong Huang

who disappeared from Shanghai and whose body,
his brother believes, is now on display in New York City
in an exhibition of plastinated cadavers

In some province a hemisphere from here
you tapped at your grandmother's kneecap, her elbow
crooked in bags of bok choy, bamboo shoots,

and rapeseed oils. You shouldered her skins
of bean curd all the way back to market,
offered coins from your pocket up

toward a farmhand she paltered for bargains.
Of you and that day, your brother remembers
this most: how your diaphragm shook as if sorry

for the quick of her tongue. How each capillary
and joint grieved the reach of her teeth. And he swears
he sees your red wince in the subway ads,

this bus stop poster where you have become a mannequin
of tendons, a mock Thinker pumped with tinctures
and phosphorescent balms, cured,

desiccated in silicon gas. Your flayed fist
against a mandible, your brother lays hands
on your knuckles. He traces aloud

the syllables of your given name. Imagines
the sound of a boy's now ossified heart.

Aftermaths

What the rains bring are trains, shorted, held fast
to bridges between stops, boots, fireworks
called off again. They say the city—mist-
figured, flood-drummed—has wanted this for weeks
and point to maps, cold sweeps, shifting pressure
along the Arthur Kill up and out to
the Sound. But Friday was free of thunder,
wind, downed lines. You smoked on the front stoop
and she walked her dog and I felt a sting
at my shin from the salt and sweat in my
stitches. We talked too long about small things—
prom nights, driftwood, punch lines to jokes poorly
translated—and had to remind ourselves
why we were here. That sky. Your son. Those grins.

        ••

We are here because of that sky, those grins
and grudges our sons will inherit if
not for us. Beneath Chambers the walls
are made with eyes, cracked tesserae of
sight lines dusted gray. Above, my wife walks
to work past picket-men, Gadsden flags, boys
arm in arm, posing beside full-color mock-
ups of Memorial Voids and storey
15 cradled by fog. Everyone stares
at everything else. It is what we know
now, how we tell each other we survive
upright in an America we own.
But suppose I'm given no piece of your
"we," you say—suppose your "home" smacks of war.

..

You say: *There was no time when home and war*
could be kept apart or held untroubled.
Take how each drive out in the Pinelands would
feel like crossing the Mason-Dixon or
how the white kids massed in pickups with their
empties and ropes, barreled into town dead-
set on catching her with him, hand-in-hand.
Now when I think about it, my mother

is who I see. She spent her nights brushing
my hair, tracing my eyes. In the mirror,
she pointed, I named: "black," "almond." Mom made
sure to add "blessed," "lucky," and I believed
her then. I've learned my son is still too young
to wonder where we're from or what we are.

..

And before you ask: I've learned what we are
is unwanted, marked by sighs and curses
like some new kind of rot. Each summer since
and every floodlit, bone-shaded Never
Forget has arrived dressed with teeth, flags, their
sight of me that night below Myrtle, fists-
in-pockets, unsure of where to run. Boys
that drunk mean what they promise and could care
less about the color of your passport
or where you call home. Fuck remembering
their way. If we let them, soon all we'll have
left are anthems, this looping montage of
eagles and bugles and smoke. Remembering—
I need you to know—takes names, faces ghosts.

••

I need you to know I've tried. To name ghosts,
to face them, dark as they are, slurred in with
the city's glossed clots and fresh buttresses,
that earthworks' trill we've let pass for rebirth—
it's to ask mercy from all that survives
us. And, yes, it's how we'll skin their myths, right
those mouths rhyming "bruise" with "brick," "break" with "leave."

Last night, stalled near Rector, I thought about
the sound of particulate matter and
burnt bone upon glass, about my brother
who refuses to shake it off. My hands
fell, emptied. I thought to knuckles, sutures,
"Go Home" cut into cheeks, how—weighted by
their marrow—flightless birds want the sky.

God Particles

The man in the pew in front of ours turned to the man on his right and
kissed him on the mouth. There in the unfinished cathedral, before blood
and body from wine and leavened bread. Before we made the sign of peace
and hummed into our pressed palms, *Now and at the hour of our death.*

••

Before Lapu-Lapu's men found him
a grave, Magellan drank rum straight
from the casks, paced the deck of his caravel,
and licked his thumb, pressing it
to the prevailing winds.

Earlier that morning, three days
after passing through the straits of All Saints
and naming the ocean after peace, the captain
knelt for the Virgin, ordered his men to sharpen
the end of a cross they will plant into the rocks.

••

October night, typhoon. The houses, candle-lit, glow like the yellow
eyes of crows. I think of delivery, hollow cries, bones to be found
and sorted into strange, precise skeletons. Before I knew
you, we slept with our heads pointing north. You said

Our dreams will rivet us, atop the shallow of our mattress and *I've already
cleaned the bathroom* and *Yes, Death is beneath us, and all these stars
are dead so it's above us, too.* Through the narrow, snaking stone gully
at the end of the street, you kissed me under my sweater

and you held me and I sunk you a little. Tell me I can
be bloody. Tell me in your family the veins go first
finding alternate routes, pulling back the tide stranded,
luminous as eyes, and I will weigh us down with cod bones stuck to a skillet
coated with grease. I will speak of visitation—a dead sister
come as a beekeeper or my finger tapping yours.

..

Whether by galleon or caravel,

St. Francis Xavier made landfall in Malacca
and met a boy named Anger,

who pleaded to be saved.

It was in his eyes—all along Anger's skin,
which spoke of an archipelago ripe with idols,
a distant continent plagued by gods.

And so Francis christened him with water,
thumbed a cross to his forehead in oil and balsam,
and lifted Pablo de Santa Fe from the lake.

..

Hear those few survivors at the dune-edge
        of the Namib Desert, those men run aground

on the Skeleton Coast, beside a trireme's broken masts
        or a carrack's open ribs, praying against the surf.

Imagine whaling ships weighted with fat and bone
        and ambergris, the crew in the shadow of these wrecks

watching springbok in their herds, living on thorns alone,
        drinking from drift-clouds with a flick of the tongue.

..

Miles beneath Geneva the men dig
with shovels and picks, churn
the bedrock with tumblers and water-

drills. Soon, tunnels will run
beneath the Jura watershed
into France, will be held

together with pipes and bolts,
supercooled magnets in triplet
arrays. There will be beams

of light, diodes in measured pulses.
If the God particle exists, they promise,
we will hold it—there, in the instant

between nothingness and mass.

2

Whatever your end may be, accept my amazement.
May I stand until death forever at attention
for any your least instruction or enlightenment.
I even feel sure you will assist me again, Master of
   insight & beauty.

JOHN BERRYMAN, "Eleven Addresses to the Lord"

All Souls' Day

Cementerio del Norte, Pagasa

Here see the city of makeshift things:
ramshackle balustrades, stopgap pipes,

clotheslines of staples and twine.
What surer proof of the risen Christ

than this tomb-stacked city,
its lungs of bamboo. Gravestone town of scaffolds

and cellophane. Smoke-heft of burnt plastic,
of tin, match-lit ranges of ash. Where bouquets

we once tied to your name, tight
with ribboned silks and rubber bands,

now wilt on their shopfronts, soak
in rainwater and lime. Where blushed with dusts

they tag wintergreen chiclets, pat rice cakes
glazed with syrup, pour Coke

into Ziploc bags all to hawk at the gates.
Lola, how warm their altars are. How their

noon-carved chancels rust in the sun and your
rosary-necked Pietà, *narra*-husk and polish

brushed smooth by their palms and kisses, rests
as we left it: bathed in novenas, an incense of coughs.

Despedida

Angat, Bulacan

Next door the men are laughing, wiping their hands
and knives against their jeans. They tap San Miguel
to San Miguel and drink to the suckling pig,
to the spit sharpened and warm over coals. My father

is there, among them, watching it bleed out, catching
what pours from its throat in a pail to save for our farewell
dinner, for the stew of innards and vinegar
my brother, my sister, and I will feed to the dogs

instead of tasting. When the squeals weaken, every man
except my father lights his first morning cigarette. They raise
a fresh beer, toast to their clutch upon a jeepney's rails
from the province into the city, to *at gagawin namin ang*

katungkulan namin. With gamecocks kicking at their pens, crowing
at the sun, my father lifts his eyes to this window, then looks away.

Sacramental

Because her left side has left her   Because lancets at the thigh, in thin veins of the arm, flesh
of her fingertips   Because her meters lap up what little blood each time

Because nutritionists, rheumatologists   Because pills and syringes arrive next-day air   Because
the patella creaks harbored in fluids, is run aground on an anchorage of bone

Because soy milk over oats each morning   Because his medicated aorta, a history of tumors
and kidneys that fail   Because he must nurse his shoulder after everything and hides it   Because gauze

Because alcohol preps   Because her hips buckle up stairs   Because his embrace is now also a crutch

And if I am to them a mirror now   If they say *anak* instead of calling my name   If my father
kisses my face as I arrive, must always kiss me when I leave

If I ever think of their living will   If coffins and lilies, last speeches and the Anointing of the Sick   If
I cannot forget which thickening eye the doctors cut into, the *Yes* above her left

If then canopic jars, funerary urns, a sabeline daub of rouge across his nostrils   If I notice a scapular
caught on a collar, the St. Jude novena in her pocket

If we pray for some guarantee of heaven, a patron saint for hopeless causes

Socorro

Grandma's skin the color of chestnuts cracked
open by mouth and her handing me the flesh
inside. Pulling at the skin around her knuckles
I marveled at its give, its smell of Parliaments,
its thinness like rice paper.

Every day she dared me to arm wrestle, tapping
the mattress to her left, rubbing
the sheets in concentric circles, clearing-
off an arena for our elbows.

Her right palm always shrouded mine, always
gave a little before the kill, before I had to wheel
the oxygen tank closer to her side of the bed. She would pull
the elastic band back so I could slide my face
into the mask, so I could breathe
what she breathed—her laughing
as I coughed up only air.

2.

When Grandpa woke from dreaming of his wife
dead for twelve years by now,

he made the sign of the cross
against his chest, sat on the edge of his bed,

and listened to a fan push air into a corner
which seemed, that morning, sharp with lizards.

He made no mention of the house duster she wore
in last night's vision, its straps loose at the shoulders or

how his wife propped her right elbow up with her left fist,
ashes in her knuckles, an unfiltered cigarette at her lips.

At breakfast, Grandpa watched the dogs gnaw
at their leashes, gave us only what Grandma sang

to him all night: *Nakalimutan mo na ako.* You
have already forgotten me.

Blessing the Animals

We have gathered up animals on this feast of St. Francis
to be blessed. In a parking lot beside the church, cleared
save for bales of hay and traffic horses, the goats

and llamas from the petting zoo a town over
are chewing at their cords, the camels' necks hung
with scapulae. The Elks and Legion men have leashed

border collies to terriers, will garland parakeets with rosaries.
They hold house cats in their arms. Our Monsignor crosses
himself in front of a statue of Jesus and His Most Sacred

Heart, beside the flagpole where I learned to pledge allegiance,
where I will later fold the stars and stripes into triangles
to lock up in the headmaster's desk. Next month, on my dare,

Howie will throw a bottle of Wite-Out at Christ's face, break-
off every finger on the Lord's right hand except his third.

Confluences

Because you will not talk
about your mother's hands

or describe further the meat
of her left thumb almost gone

as if eaten down to the bone,
and because it is too early yet

to imagine your mother's breast
brushed with prep gauze, held

in some nameless palm,
an attendant knuckle *There*

to mark just above her nipple, we run
along the piers, coughing

at the near-spectacle of Edgewater,
its lights adrift in the river

between here and New Jersey.
If only we could say something

about the beauty afforded to us
by distance and the prospect of loss

instead of spitting at pigeons
and kicking at wastebins. If only

there was something else but pictures
in my skull—these images of antibodies

and magnets in solution, a doctor's vow
to take arms in *the half-life*

of whatever we have to finish it off.
When you gesture at a trash barge,

the sea gulls in their furious circles, I see
a convocation above the heaps,

white cells gathering at the tips
of all her cooled syringes.

Traps

Scatter poison across a plate and slide
dish and all beneath the edge of an overturned wastebin
where a mouse is trapped. Tell yourself
there is no other way. Think of your wife who needs her peace.

Watch it first taste, then strike at the bait. Rest assured
the animal will eat whatever you feed it,
even these peppercorns flash-dyed turquoise. Imagine

the promise of *cholecalciferol*—of rock salt
at the veins when swallowed, of leech-jaws
onto bones. Imagine an overdose on your own
marrow. Sleep on how that death must feel.

Next day expect to meet in your living room nothing
but a tuft of fur, a segmented tail limp
and meaningless. Know swift darts of its calcium
still pierce the valves of its heart.

Tap the wire mesh with your right foot, test
your trap. Curse chemicals and the mouse
bounding toward you. Remember another trash can
in the kitchen. Fill it full with water

from the shower. Show the animal
what you have made for it before you combine the two.
When you check on things, note the kicking, its claw at the sides
as if to escape a flood. Forget its eyes
sinking as beads, as baubles.

On Transfiguration

Like fresh creation, it's about thresholds:
the right to name, accidentally, a
bestiary of the sea, the widow
owning a pair of moons, the chimera
of subway and daughter. That stars explode,
that someone's dropped a load of pipes on the
concrete, that in all this heat and shadow,
we agree we are born again—lava-
like, Lazarus-like—into the known world.
That we live here is beautiful sometimes
because we believe we forget these cells
called "home" for the chance at resurrection.
So what is it we've saved? Skull? Soul? Vulture?
Maybe this earth, turned in on itself and made.

..

The marsh across the street, the woman I
made love to last night: iridescent wings
from distant ancestral species. Finding
bruise-glossed feathers, I wonder about ice
and rock, our blood tuned to iron, the mind
in some quantum trick. These circulating
fringes create us and hold the wanting
together. We think. We need.   To survive
is to cross and graft to cultivar, but
I don't understand why that impulse feels
like air and extinction. After the fact
I can't recall the rest of the story.
I preserve loss with venom and a nest
of Barbary doves. I want you to want me.

..

Making it through unaltered is the point
in matters of remorse. Be calm. Soon
we will bear sentimentality, scent
what is lost in these cells with carrion,
asphodel, turpentine, forsythia
blooming somewhere in the dark. Scientists
warn & call this consequence: black huia
perished but for museum specimens,
the great auks beaten, dashed, the auger birds
coated with fallout. *Everything will go*
to wrack, they say. *The thriving, delighted,*
and everything keeping Him close to you.
Scored for human voices, a body is
the morning before opening my eyes.

Divination

1.

As though bleeding blackbirds, the grove
changed colors. We watched the flock's pitch
and tremble from the colonnade,
pointed at wings and their fluid graft
upon the afternoon. The basilica ruins bare,
surrounded by scatter grass. The vault
nothing but sky. You said I crossed myself
by the Revelator's tomb just before faint-
ing at your feet. I heard a guide near the grave
swear St. John never died but sleeps beneath
us, breathing up dust where the apse
would have held the sacristy. Without
words I came to and you cupped water
to my mouth and I asked you if it was over.

2.

How many times have you heard me tell
the one where I stand before the assembly,
a mouth of mercury, a set of gums lined with caulk

and stegosaurus plates? Or that other, where my knees
become the rim of a sink and me looking into
a mirror, watching my teeth fall out

scoring the bowl with their roots? So
tell me what this means: these past few nights I
was a skull glazed with camphor, then a row

of carrion birds refusing a sky burial's
first offerings. I was *Middlemarch*
enacted with marionettes and wine

barrels, a watercolor mock-up of a church
burned to the ground. I was a jaw—
in and out of its ball socket—

chewing without end.

3

Now I am ready to tell how bodies are changed
Into different bodies.

TED HUGHES, "Creation; Four Ages; Flood; Lycaon"

Antipodal

To get here from there takes longer than you
think, a faith in cardinal directions

and magnetic north. Watch for the trench-blue
of the caldera, the lychee and knives

lining the shoulder of the road. If you
pass harvests of wasp nests or hear swallows

in the hawthorns, you've gone too far. Keep to
the viaduct span. Ignore the exits.

Take a left past the community pools
fenced with concertina wire, rock doves

pulled by rival winds. Like venom all through
the arteries, rumble and thrum to this

island of mirrors and fingernail ends—
this rat king city of anvils and blinds.

In the dead of winter we

In the dead of winter we
slid forward toward corner bus stops shifting
our weight with the flapping of mittens.

Like as how water is
water first   then snow
then ice,
our fingers too shifted states:
going from peace signs to rabbit ears back
behind each other's bonnets to too-
wide rests for invisible cigarettes—
        How we would grip at our bottom lips, pucker
then hoot into the pinks of each other's cheeks,
            remember?

And
weren't we always so surprised by the crispness
of our bangs frozen solid—frozen black
into points?

Here tonight the breeze off the Hudson tastes like fireplaces
and my face is tight with the surprise that air
        in its invisibilities
can still pinch
and slash
like that
        like this

taking everything I can muster
Walking face first into the avenues toward home
and the hiss
of our radiator, which has soldered itself
to the highest heats

Ballast

The winds and all the many millions
of days have thrust themselves against
us. See how heavy our breastbones
weigh against the air, how our marrow
lacks the pores that might allow us
even a single, buoyant bound
into the sky. We have arms where
wings should reside, blood thickened with
brine and iron. We are the lump sum
of the ground who holds us dear. And
yet, there are the equatorial
calms begging to be breached. And there
is the cusp of a canyon dressed
in a coronal of marigolds
visible only from above.

 ..

Save your blessed fires, your blessed salts,
nectarine devotionals spiced
for starboard altars. The tenders

and trawlers mothballed and dry-docked
want more of us than prayer beads
and weeping, snake wine and raveling

nets. But what can we offer save
for harvests of rust, black kites, signs
of the cross? Each morning the gulf

between promise and wound flares like
a ghost limb, a tunnel filling
slowly with salt water and krill.

We are a hive of nerves—yes, a
flotilla raided by the dark.

..

Cormorants strut the pier lengths
without notice of dive teams

and boatmen, winches heavy with
what's left of the rear rotors, seam-

welds, the guidance surfaces
frayed and buckled. *Not the dark of*

water, but its force upon us,
a spokesman will mouth

into boom mics, naming the enemy
and its hold upon tenders

marshaled to the wrecks. Call it recovery
when the river surrenders

all that remains from its silt, when a plane
is found whole *with the exception of wings.*

As the river crests, mud-rich with forgotten things

Colors this summer Raritan
carries: of this flailing, flaring New
      Jersey sunset   of the burnt-ends of cigarettes
as they   and gravity   then the river kiss
      Red's surge toward night-
fall: a dark diastole   rich with the blood
      of pigeons, worms, catfish—a mercury blood,
heavy with gas   This orange Raritan
      This drunk, Dutch princess   flanked as if by knights:
trunks bent, leadened with her forgotten things   they knew
      tomorrow would bring nothing   but kisses
of moss   feasts of cigarettes
      and pistols, denim and pulp   All sick at rest
with clay in the roots, their shallowed blood,
      bruised corpuscles kiss
only the light left, only the ache   for some life rarer than
      this, apart from the current's slurs and weights   New
moon—pulsing yellow muscle of the night-
      to-be—flexes along each surface: driftwood night-
stands, a kingdom of algae, ash-nests of cigarettes—
      even the vertebrae of gulls aglow   as henna-brown canoe
hulls course past blood
      oranges, pockets of glass, a Samaritan
mold   And as the bitter, mosquito kiss

      of evening ebbs in, its shifts and shadows kiss
every branch, every veined leaf and weed: night-
      shade, poison oak, sumac root   orangutan
vines of ivy along the banks awash in cigarette
      fog, ripe with tar   And now as how blood

clots to black, the river thickens tints: its platelets of news-
      paper ink   shake-songs of newt
throats and cricket shanks kissing
      the growing murk   Here Freon blood's

systolic pump through fridge coils, these night-
        sticks beached among trestles, cigarettes'
leach and slush: all lullaby the muck   This Raritan—

        this hematite sinew   moth-swollen nightingale
ventricle kissed with charcoals, cigarette
        papers—its blood-dyed roar, return

Drifting toward the bottom, Jacques Piccard recalls the sky

Hour #4, hadal zone—*Forgive*
me. I can only think of chainmaille for
a fitting match to this die-cast shade of
black outside our porthole. It is far more
deep a nothingness than that. So pure a
cold that our floodlights appear to burn as
stars do. What words can render void, this nova
of mercury bulbs through the clear abyss?

Our descent was marked by medusae, clouds
of shrimp, luminescent matter adrift
on ambient currents. No such flares and
flashes at these fathoms. Don says we passed
the basement of twilight hours ago,
likens the dark to a murder of crows.

••

Bathyscaphe *Trieste*, Mariana Trench,
23 Jan.—*I have heard how Iceland's*
sunlight trickles away by minutes each
fall so that, by the solstice, darkness spans
8/10 of the day. I cannot divine
living without sight of the sky for so
long and here must admit relief that fine
fissures now run the face of our window.
It means we must cut our stay at the Deep
to minutes in case the pressures decide
to gnaw at the hull itself. It means we
should thank the Good Lord for lime-hydroxide,
for Father's gondola lifted miles above
Augsburg, breaching the air, buoyant as doves.

••

13:06, gauges mark seven miles
deep—*To settle here atop the trench floor*
is to kick up grackles from their perches,
to run headlong into rooks on the tor
and to watch their wings overcome the sky.

All around us seems an empire at the
height of its forces, a tuber of night
and ooze, bone fog and soot we come to love
because we can. Don and I lack the room
to embrace. We arrive without cornet
or flag. There is something like an anthem
in my marrow so let us sound this last
fathom out with it. Let us trawl the dark
for whale fall, sing of our ballast like larks.

Corpus

Paris, 1786

When the Cemetery of Saints Innocents
could no longer hold the coming bodies
or sustain its stacks of bones strewn

with soot and heirloom curios,
its obelisks engraved with psalms
or given names in hollow-relief,

the gravediggers raised fences
to surround the plots and their
compound dead. By decree

and plank and nail, the gathered masses
were turned away, told to wait for word
of better tombs. The mourners

with their hymnal flowers, their spangled
cadence, their butcher paper and chalks
barred from the grounds to make room

for shovels and barrows, the horse-carts
loaded full with all manner of skulls
and joints. Beyond the city walls,

watching his quarries deepened
and mapped, lined with generations
of teeth and arms, Lenoir confesses

to the catacomb ledgers: *If
I did not move them, our dead
would overtake us all.*

Vanitas

With braided line through dorsal fins, pierced
through cartilage and denticles, the artist suspends
the Requiem shark in solution, makes of it
a triptych in aqua blue formaldehyde.

In a gallery overlooking the park, a field
trip circles the tank, carries drawing pads
and soft charcoals. Light refracts, breaks
the great fish into a shiver of parts.

Cast in this sunset thickened
by the glass, two of the children compare
sketches: her shark devours a diving bell
whole. His night swimmer stares
straight up into a whitewater throat.

What the bones tell us

Of a child before the trepan, trill
of the stone pick, the shaman's loosening of the blood-
swell against her skull   Of hands
as a poultice, the woundwort salve
at the forehead   Of a burial with cornflower garland   Of joints still-
nursed with pollen still among her bones we find here circled

by bones   That mothers wove their fingers raw   That eldermen farmed
the cordillera with palm and knuckle   That boys cast atlatl
and dart even with shoulders broken at the center places, would walk
and fight on fractured legs, with bruised marrow

         That when the Inca
crossed into the cloud forest so also came the new
dead dried, bound together as bundles, skin and eyes intact,
arrayed in feathers and shells for the soul to follow

         ··

Berlin *Archaeopteryx*, bird-
         lizard, the claw ringed by feathers,
the jaw bearing teeth   Hollow wish-

         bone vault within salt-stone, engraved
arabesque, a *grand jeté* crowned
         with sickle wrist   *Urvogel*, lathe-

tendon, pressed Tethys lithograph,
         a counterslab print of thresholds
down in the lagoon bed, waiting—

         Icarus somersault, snake-neck
Mephistopheles Delacroix
         drafts nude-winged above Wittenberg,

between the earth and air   Rock-speak
         confluence of demon, of law

··

We are left the bull
or bison or auroch, its charge

across the Lascaux triptych
and the rhinoceros unfinished

Here a man without bones
is a box with the head of a bird

Iconoclasts

Because they cannot pray
to faces and no mother
or man can be seen as God
they have taken this baptistery
altarpiece—the Virgin Mary
veiled in ultramarine, the infant
Christ water-gilded gold
onto black poplar—and bound
it up with hides and sinew
string, weighted it with rubble
and quarry rocks to heave
into the Bosphorus. In the rock
churches they have likewise found
eyes and mouths to be scratched
away, their fingernails tearing
at John the Beloved, their tamarisk
branches sharpened, burnt
to scar the Pantocrator, his hand,
as a blessing, spread across the vault.

Invocation

1. DAVENPORT, IOWA

Let them have Varanasi, Lord.
Allow them their ghats and barges,
their boatmen hauling sandalwood,
pyres thick with bones. Give the Ganges
over with Samarra, Qom, Al-
Hillah. Gift them cypress and grave-
plot incense, their minarets' call
and alarum smoke. Guard Your name

from curses, Lord, let tongues, cornets
wrest back our continent, make of
us bayonet and vestibule, Western
Front and Temple Mount. How this Earth
halves for You if You will it, arms
us with throats for the coming drums.

2. HOLOFERNES, TO JUDITH AT THE STRIKE

"... *Give me strength this day, O Lord God of Israel!"*
And she struck his neck twice with all her might.

JUDITH 13:7–8

We—cast into this pall, this tenebrae,
bound up by throat's clot, hair's shock, eye's seizure,
sweat's canker—are not different. We obey,
sacrifice, widow and mete—now, unsure.

      How can it be that these gods we love call
me to bleed prone on my sheets? Douse duty
with wine's headiness, your jasmine taste?—Pull
us into the reek of my marrow? See
how in their own name we invade and rend,
divine their wants, must back each falchion's
hack with a loll of commandments, this bend
and fracture of verse. We—twist, collision,
torch and scabbard—pawn our breaths in this place—
this dark—perfumed with cedar, wreathed in gauze.

Countless nights I have known this same gaze still-
born on a phalanx of men. Through spaces
between fingers, back behind palms' failed shields,
their eyes   as these: hollowed, cast in salts, full-
frieze of silica, ash—black, cracked marble
mouths with their absence of teeth.   Know: hell is

not the wince, twist, sickle-hiss of asps' tails
at the skull, nor is it our cheeks' shocked cull—
this atrophy of screams.   Hell is memory

lost: how hearts, wounds, gasps will clot to stone just
kouros pale or stelae blank   and on and
on.   You, bare of laurels, and me—memory
gone of my hair soft, sweet with hyacinth—
never loved, choked in his necklace of hands.

4. ON THE SIXTH DAY, UGOLINO THINKS OF HIS CHILDREN

Poscia, più che 'l dolor, poté 'l digiuno.
DANTE, *Inferno* XXXIII, l. 75

Little Anselmo is already gone.

Even without sight of him near my feet,
my ankles bound with fetters, I have known
his dying each day. Nino will be next.

Each grip on my thigh falls colder, each breath
fainter still along these shallowed ribs.—I

cannot answer them—cannot father
more grief here among what remains alive,
knots itself around my waist, fastens to my
knees: the arms' fevered grope, guts' churn and plea
for bread, meat. When they saw my agony,

heard my bite grinding knuckles against teeth,
fingers chewed to bone, these boys rose, begged: *undress
us of this flesh you gave.*   Wept: *eat of us.*

The one that you must notice is never
the angel's pointing   Wordless, mouthless, sleek
through my father's jawline covered over
by the bloom of gray, black, through to the bleat
of the waiting ram   Nor should what matters be
the flexed clamp at Father's furrowed wrist, those
terse, thin, new from the God machinery

And, for certain, forget the weapon: lose
his first finger curling the blade, his hilt
to deflect my inevitable spray
Lose his four unseen   nails deep, digging, willed
free into my neck. For its rosary
taste against the teeth, *remember the thumb*:
wet, pressing, leathered by the Canaan sun.

They will find us on these tapes years
from now, our dancing and toasts, our
opening of gifts. They will ask us

how we ever allowed ourselves
to look so young, to live without
knowing what they now take for fact.

They will point and laugh at us—our
names for each other, the exact
announcements of time. So many

volumes of this. So many reels
and adaptors, converters and
discs. We will translate before they

say they cannot make sense of it.

After this, Loving Kindness and Asanga flew

for Phebus Etienne

These church gates are locked, like yesterday,
        and so I have not yet prayed
for you the right way, knelt in your memory, offered
        intentions or lit chapel candles in your name.

When John told me, I was an avenue away,
        reading on a gallery wall about Asanga,
who wanted Loving Kindness to meet him in a cave, who waited
        and waited to talk enlightenment over Assam tea.

On that painted cotton, he wears a halo of mineral malachite,
        is clothed in a dye of ground cinnabar, is flanked by the story
of his life. This is what I know now about the upper-right corner,
        where a miniature Asanga flies

with the found bodhisattva and both float buoyant without need
        for pinion feathers or ailerons, where they are weightless,
steering toward paradise with just their robes and arms:
        Loving Kindness and Asanga flew to the Tushita heaven.

It is what I was trying to understand before I took John's call
        and he asked if I had heard about your passing
days ago, alone in your apartment, most likely from a collapse
        of the heart. It is what happens after Asanga lifts

Loving Kindness up and carries him through town on his back,
        the townspeople blind, as always, to the beatitudes among them.

Mine will be a beautiful service

1.

When you bury me, fold
my arms, neat

over the plateau
of a double-breasted suit,

the angle of the lapel
matching my now

permanent expression.
Pressed, chemical

I will look content,
but confused,

as when you watched me turn
in my sleep, dreaming:

      of a Golgotha
in beeswax, a coffin

for swallows, a toothless augur
reading the flights and cries

of owls. You
will hear the cadence

of my voice, the snapping
oblique of my laugh. Among the votives

and canticles, you will trace,
with the tips of your thumbs,

lines of demarcation
between the fallow of my scalp

and the dunes of my forehead.
Quiet, you will paste

stray hairs back
into their place.

All sod and taproot now, all bulb
and tuber and stemshoot   Mulch throb,
lush with worms and slugs—we are never worth
more than this

Thrum of the earth, clatter-bulge of cicada shells
along a coffin's hinges   Teak and scented cedar
flushed with compost   An elegy
of rot, this counterfeit reliquary

     If you each day clutch
our pillows, press them to your face, pray
to take in some atom of me all
into the hollows of your chest, yes

I promise my ghost will find you
should you want someone else to love

SACRUM

L. 4–6   From Book 1, Chapter 18 of Andreas Vesalius' *De Humani Corporis Fabrica*, where the anatomist wonders about the traditional nomenclature of the coccyx and sacrum: "It is unclear why they called it 'sacred,' unless they called it so from its rare appearance and shape, or because it so resembles a divine bulwark, or . . . because it is grand and spacious, as we think Troy, the sea, hunger, and such like are called 'sacred' by the poets."

L. 44   In Tagalog, *barangay* refers to a small community or village. In *A History of the Philippines: From Indios Bravos to Filipinos* (The Overlook Press, 2010), Luis H. Francia extends the definition, noting the word's origins in *balangay*, "the outriggered seafaring vessels of the pre-colonial Philippines, on which a family or clan traveled."

L. 54–55   In Book 1, Chapter 5, Vesalius asserts that "the human head is formed for the sake of the eyes," which, in turn, need "the soft nerves of the brain." All of these sensory forms depend upon a vanguard of bone because "if they extend too far all soft things are soon pulled apart, broken, or damaged."

TELEMACHY

The title is taken from the name often given to the first four books of Homer's *Odyssey*, in which Odysseus' son, Telémakhos, leaves Ithaka to find word of his father's life or death.

L. 9   St. Telemachus, also known as Almachus, was a monk whose violent death supposedly influenced the end of gladiatorial games in Rome. Saint Theodoret of Cyrrhus writes, "When the admirable emperor [Honorius] was informed of [Telemachus' death by stoning], he numbered Telemachus in the number of victorious martyrs, and put an end to that impious spectacle." His feast day is celebrated on January 1.

L. 20–37   The Kill Sparrow War, or the Great Sparrow Campaign, was a part of an official initiative known as the Four Pests Campaign, which sought to eliminate rats, flies, mosquitoes, and sparrows from China. Begun in 1958 as a prime directive from Mao Zedong himself, the drive called on both children and adults to besiege the bird's natural breeding grounds with noisemakers, scarecrows, and weapons. Sparrows starved to death or suffered heart attacks from prolonged flight. With their natural predators all but eliminated, locusts flourished, eating their way through the very crops the Sparrow War promised to protect. The subsequent famine killed millions.

GOD PARTICLES

L. 5–6 The phrase "Before Lapu-Lapu's men found him / a grave" originally appeared in "Shoals," a poem by Jon Pineda.

L. 15–28 This sonnet is composed of lines and images taken from the poetry of Alessandra Trinidad, Jessica Flynn, Alison Moncrief Bromage, Amber West, Mrigaa Sethi, Anna McDonald, and Sassy Ross.

L. 39–46 Despite unforgiving currents and severe topography, the western coast of Namibia is revered by indigenous San bushmen. They know it as the Land God Made in Anger.

ALL SOULS' DAY

L. 16 *Lola* is a Tagalog word meaning "grandmother."

L. 18 *Narra* is a Philippine rosewood valued for its innate luster and natural fragrance.

DESPEDIDA

The title comes from the Spanish for "farewell." In the Philippines, a *despedida* is a traditional dinner or celebration held in honor of someone who is going away.

L. 12–13 As both promise and admonition, *Gawin nyo ang katungkulan nyo at gagawin namin ang katungkulan namin* translates from Tagalog to mean "You do your duty and we'll do ours."

SACRAMENTAL

L. 8 A term of endearment, the Tagalog word *anak* can be loosely translated to mean "my child."

TRAPS

L. 8 Cholecalciferol is a chemical variant of vitamin D3 used in rodenticides. Upon ingestion, the victim's body begins to produce and absorb toxic levels of calcium from its own body. Death occurs from severe hypercalcemia.

ON TRANSFIGURATION

These recombinant sonnets emerge from crossing poems in Colin Cheney's *Here Be Monsters* (The University of Georgia Press, 2010) with work from Kimiko Hahn's *Toxic Flora* (W. W. Norton, 2010).

BALLAST

L. 56 The phrase "hive of nerves" is taken from the title of an essay by Christian Wiman, originally published in the summer 2010 edition of *The American Scholar*.

L. 71 The italicized phrase is adapted from an August 14, 2009, press release from the National Transportation Safety Board that describes the salvage of debris from a sightseeing helicopter and an airplane that collided over the Hudson River.

DRIFTING TOWARD THE BOTTOM, JACQUES PICCARD RECALLS THE SKY

On January 23, 1960, accompanied by Lt. Don Walsh of the U.S. Navy, Jacques Piccard survived a prolonged descent into the Challenger Deep, the deepest trench in the ocean floor. Their submersible, the *Trieste*, incorporated the life's work of Auguste Piccard, famed physicist, stratospheric balloonist, and Jacques' father.

VANITAS

After Damien Hirst's conceptual piece, *The Physical Impossibility of Death in the Mind of Someone Living*.

WHAT THE BONES TELL US

L.1–14   These lines make reference to the rituals, burial practices, and family structures of the Chachapoya, a pre-Columbian civilization that lived in the cloud forests of present-day Peru. The invasion of the Inca occurred sometime in the late fifteenth century.

L. 15–28   And these lines consider the Berlin Specimen of *Archaeopteryx lithographica* beside *Mephistopheles in Flight over Wittenberg*, a lithograph by Eugène Delacroix.

L. 29–34   The "Lascaux triptych" refers to Paleolithic cave paintings discovered in 1940 in southwestern France. This particular scene can be found in a section, or room, of the caves known as the Shaft of the Dead Man.

DAVENPORT, IOWA

On October 11, 2008, Rev. Arnold Conrad delivered the opening prayer at a campaign rally for Sen. John McCain. Conrad's invocation seemed to envision the U.S. presidential race as a battle between those "gathered here today in Jesus's name" and those of other faiths, who might, he imagines, "think that their god is bigger."

HOLOFERNES, TO JUDITH AT THE STRIKE

After Michelangelo Merisi da Caravaggio's *Judith Beheading Holofernes*.

MEDUSA, AT FIRST SIGHT OF HER FACE

Inspired by Michelangelo Merisi da Caravaggio's *Medusa*, an apotropaic image of the Gorgon painted onto polychrome wood.

L. 11   In his *Early Greece* (Harvard University Press, 1993), Oswyn Murray suggests that the "great series of naked male youths known as 'kouros' dominate the history of archaic sculpture [and] often stood as idealized memorials of the dead on graves."

ON THE SIXTH DAY, UGOLINO THINKS OF HIS CHILDREN

Inspired by Jean-Baptiste Carpeaux's *Ugolino and His Sons*.

In the Prairie Schooner Book Prize in Poetry series

To order or obtain more information on these or other University of Nebraska Press titles, visit nebraskapress.unl.edu.

Printed in the USA
CPSIA information can be obtained
at www.ICGtesting.com
LVHW041328240823
756152LV00005B/182